WILLIAM GLEN · VILLAGE GATHERING · 1993

Come See Our Christmas Village

by
Suzanne Larkin Kueppers

designed and illustrated
by
Gina Bugée Karl

published by
Gina B Press

Gina B Press
P.O. Box 11288
St. Paul, Minnesota 55111
(612) 452-7019

ISBN: 0-9635629-0-8

First edition
10 9 8 7 6 5 4 3 2

Printed in the
United States of America

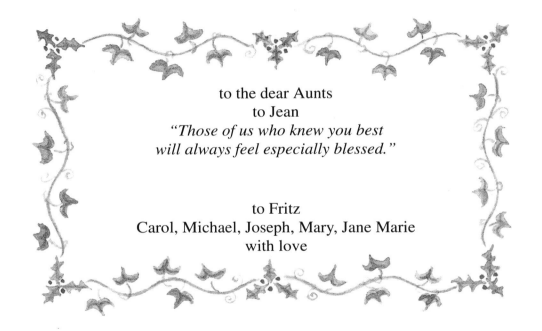

to the dear Aunts
to Jean
*"Those of us who knew you best
will always feel especially blessed."*

to Fritz
Carol, Michael, Joseph, Mary, Jane Marie
with love

Please let me tell you what a Christmas village means.
It's many tiny figures resembling city scenes.
Houses, stores and people… streets up and down…
Everything you dream of in a make-believe town…

Arrange them on a mantel or a table in the hall,
but underneath the Christmas tree is the best place of all.
Light them up like magic, and there before your eyes,
… your very own village, in miniature size.

Come See Our Christmas Village

Our dearest Nieces and Nephews,

"Come see our Christmas village," to you each year we say.

This message comes from loving aunts, aging more each day.

So this year, for the first time, we will to you impart

the story of our village…how it got its start.

As Christmas Day draws near, we dress our tree in splendor.

Then we set the village 'neath, its quiet charm to render.

Our village truly has become a precious antique treasure.

Collecting all its pieces has been a lifelong pleasure.

Dad gave Mother the schoolhouse with a dome

the Christmas they built our family home.

Later, the boys found the general store,

followed by the cottage with a bright red door.

Our brothers all married and raised you so dearly.

Both of us remained at home…adding to the village yearly.

The family gathers on Christmas, though our parents have departed.

It's an annual celebration…a tradition that they started.

Five generations have gathered close around

the tiny peaceful village that never makes a sound.

…eyed the horse and carriage…the wooden train so small,

with Santa and his reindeer in the center of it all.

Oh how fast the years go by!

"We're both in our nineties," we say with a sigh.

Our hearing is gone…our bodies are weak.

…two maiden ladies far beyond our peak.

Each year we say, "This is the last,"

to set the village as we have in the past.

Then we pause and exclaim, "Oh, my,

we must attempt just one more try."

It takes a lot of fussing to put it all in place.

Each single little character must have its rightful space.

One of us sits upon a chair, pointing her finger, "Over there."

The other crawls beneath the tree...to find that place, "just where."

After our task has been completed, and the village looks just right,

we stand and gaze at our masterpiece, filled with renewed delight.

Can you guess the real reward, what makes our spirits rise?

It is the look of wonder that lights up the children's eyes.

Our village almost comes to life

as we watch the piper holding his fife.

The houses warm up 'neath the pines standing guard

behind the picket fence surrounding the yard.

Then everything is ready…in the parlor we sit and wait

for you to come, dear family, and help us celebrate.

Our hearts dance so joyfully, as you approach the door,

and we meet in sweet confusion…at Christmas time once more.

How very still the house becomes after telling you goodbye…

the cider pot is put away, dishtowels hung to dry.

We've never thought to ask before, but now we'd like to know,

"After both of us are gone, where will our village go?"

Our blessings and our love to you,

Aunt Myrtle and Aunt Margaret, too

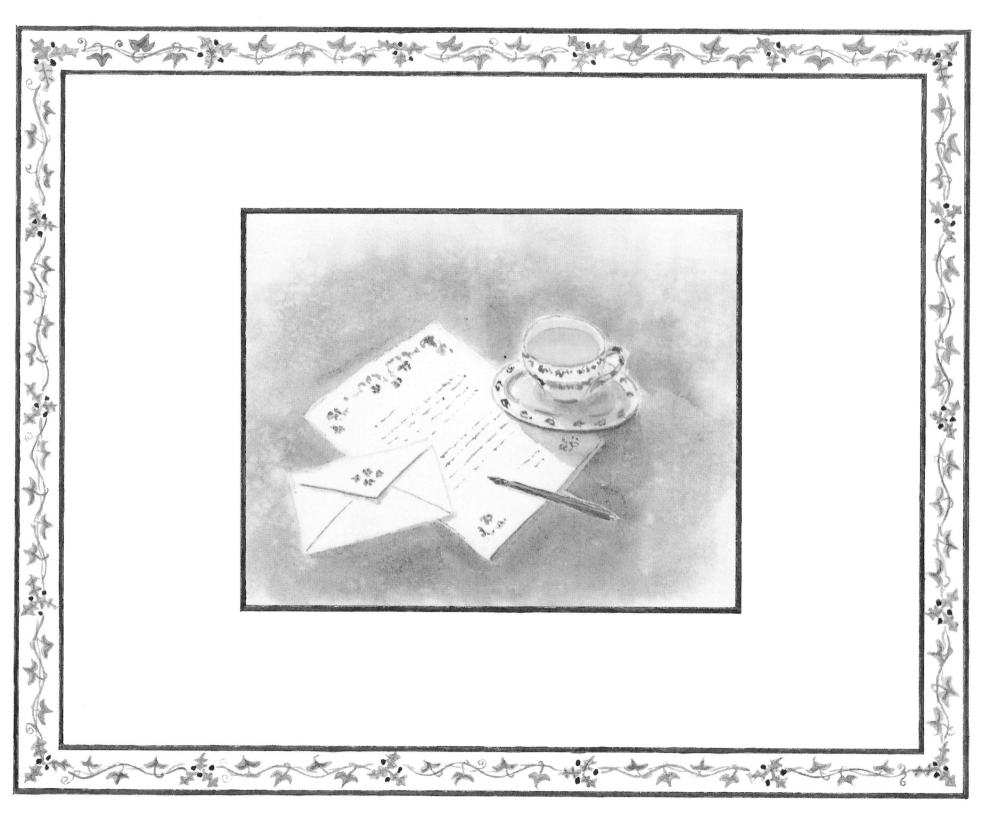

Dearest Aunt Myrtle and Aunt Margaret,

I know this message will have no reply

for we whispered to you a last goodbye.

Your letter and mine, I'm tucking away

for safekeeping, to share with loved ones someday.

After joyous farewells last Christmas night,

with visions of the village still holding tight,

memories flashed from deep inside…

mindful keepsakes, never to subside.

It was Christmas time so long ago…

We drove to your house through falling snow.

As your nephew's new bride, I was anxious to see

both of you and your Christmas tree.

Ah! That splendid tree, standing straight and tall

was keeping watch as we entered the hall.

It beckoned me close for my very first sight

of the Christmas village, showing off in the light.

The gingerbread house… the skater on ice…

the general store filled with candy and spice…

The light from the church threw a lustrous sheen

as my eyes swept across that magnificent scene.

As time went by and our family increased,

our holiday visits never did cease.

With arms full of gifts, we journeyed to you,

bringing our children… later, their children too.

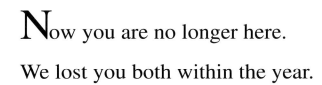

Now you are no longer here.

We lost you both within the year.

In closing up and cleaning out

the many treasures you left about,

we found all neatly set aside,

the *Christmas village!* We laughed and cried.

We gathered the pieces with loving care,

dividing them up for the families to share,

so each nephew and niece could start a collection,

while remembering yours, in smiling reflection.

Each year we'll add a piece or two,

the way you always used to do.

But the favorite one will always be

that precious heirloom from 'neath your tree.

I'll begin my village with a church display,

a handsome town hall and a horse-drawn sleigh.

…loving reminders of Christmases past,

keeping memories alive that were meant to last.

Those of us who knew you best

will always feel especially blessed,

as we cherish our villages every year anew.

Merry Christmas, sweet ladies.

Lovingly,

Sue

Acknowledgments:

Barbara Anderson-Sannes
Pauline Dahl
Bobbi Jasmin
Bill, Kelly & Thomas Karl
Vonni Senn
Elise Widen
The Christopher Inn

My very deepest appreciation.